P9-DGE-966

Northbrook Public Library
3 1123 01118 3376

DISCOVER SEA STARS

3

by Helen Foster James

Cherry Lake Publishing • Ann Arbor, Michigan

Published in the United States of America
by Cherry Lake Publishing
Ann Arbor, Michigan
www.cherrylakepublishing.com

Content Adviser: Dominique A. Didier, PhD, Associate Professor,
Department of Biology, Millersville University
Reading Adviser: Marla Conn, ReadAbility, Inc

Photo Credits: © meunierd/Shutterstock Images, cover; © Song Heming/Shutterstock Images, 4; © NatureDiver/Shutterstock Images, 6; © scubaluna/Shutterstock Images, 8; © nito/Shutterstock Images, 10; © Lee Prince/Shutterstock Images, 12; © Ethan Daniels/Shutterstock Images, 14; © Aleksei Potov/Shutterstock Images, 16; © Eugene Kalenkovich, 18; © Andaman/Shutterstock Images, 20

Library of Congress Cataloging-in-Publication Data
James, Helen Foster, 1951- author.
Discover sea stars / Helen Foster James.
pages cm.—(Splash!)
Summary: "This Level 3 guided reader introduces basic facts about sea stars, including their physical characteristics, diet, and habitat. Simple callouts ask the student to think in new ways, supporting inquiry-based reading. Additional text features and search tools, including a glossary and an index, help students locate information and learn new words."—Provided by publisher.
Audience: Ages 6–10
Audience: K to grade 3
Includes bibliographical references and index.
ISBN 978-1-63362-606-5 (hardcover)—ISBN 978-1-63362-696-6 (pbk.)—ISBN 978-1-63362-786-4 (pdf)—ISBN 978-1-63362-876-2 (ebook)
1. Starfishes—Juvenile literature. I. Title.

QL467.2.J36 2016
593.9'3—dc23

2015005588

Cherry Lake Publishing would like to acknowledge the work of the Partnership for 21st Century Skills. Please visit www.p21.org for more information.

Printed in the United States of America
Corporate Graphics

TABLE OF CONTENTS

A Sea Star's Rays

A sea star has a star shape. It has a flat body with a middle **disk**. Sea stars can be 5 to 10 inches (12.7 to 25.4 centimeters) wide in size. Sea stars usually have five arms.

A sea star has at least five arms.

When a sea star loses an arm, it can grow another. It takes about a year for a new **ray** to grow. The **detached** ray can grow a new body.

This type of sea star, a sun star, has many rays.

Sea stars have eye spots. They can see light and dark. Eye spots are at the tip of each ray. A sea star with five rays has five eye spots.

LOOK!

Look at the "eyes" on this ray. They don't look like other animals' eyes. Can you think of any other animals that have "eyes" but don't have faces?

Each ray has an eye spot on the tip.

Stars of the Sea

Sea stars have colors and patterns to help them hide. This is called **camouflage**. They hide to keep safe from **predators**.

This sea star has camouflaged itself to look like the sea floor.

Sea stars have many tiny tube feet on each of their rays. They stay safe by hanging on rocks with their feet.

By using their thousands of tube feet like suction cups, sea stars are able to hold onto rocks.

Sea stars mostly eat **mussels**, clams, and oysters. They pull the shells apart with their feet. Some sea stars will eat jellyfish.

These sea stars are eating a jellyfish.

There are many **species** of sea stars. Sea stars are also called starfish, but they are not fish. People can see and sometimes touch sea stars at **aquariums**.

Aquariums often have sea stars.

Protecting Sea Stars

You might see a sea star when the **tide** is low. Look carefully, but leave them alone.

Why is a sea star not a fish?

This sea star has climbed out of the water up onto a rock.

Some sea stars are **endangered**. **Pollution** hurts their **environment**. Keeping the oceans clean helps protect sea stars.

What can you do to protect sea stars? Go online to find out more. Are there any sea stars near where you live, or near a place you have visited?

Sea stars like this one need a clean environment to survive.

Think About It

Do you have more questions about sea stars? Go online with an adult or visit a library for more facts about sea stars.

What other animals can you see at aquariums? How are they similar to sea stars? How are they different?

What other animals can you see when the ocean's tide is low? Why do you think that is? How do you think they can survive out of the water?

Find Out More

BOOK

Halfmann, Janet. *Star of the Sea: A Day in the Life of a Starfish.* New York: Henry Holt, 2011.

WEB SITE

National Geographic Kids: Sea Star

http://kids.nationalgeographic.com/content/kids/en_US/animals/sea-star/

Read more about sea stars and look at some beautiful photos.

Glossary

aquariums (uh-KWAIR-ee-uhmz) places for visitors to see ocean animals

camouflage (KAM-uh-flahzh) how an animal blends with its surroundings

detached (dih-TACHD) removed or separated

disk (DISK) the round, flat center of a sea star

endangered (en-DAYN-jurd) at risk of dying out

environment (en-VYE-ruhn-muhnt) the natural surroundings of living things, such as the air, land, or sea

mussels (MUHS-uhl) a type of shellfish that have a black shell and can be eaten

pollution (puh-LOO-shuhn) the act of polluting or the state of being polluted

predators (PRED-uh-turz) animals that live by hunting other animals for food

ray (RAY) an arm of a sea star

species (SPEE-sheez) one type, or kind, of an animal

tide (TIDE) the rising and falling of the ocean

Index

About the Author

Dr. Helen Foster James likes to read, travel, and volunteer as a naturalist interpreter in the mountains with her friends. When the tide is low, she likes to go to tide pools with her friends and look for sea stars. She lives by the Pacific Ocean in San Diego, California, with her husband, Bob.